LEARN
TOGETHER

NUMBER WORK 2
Number lines, ordering, simple addition

Sandra Soper

A Piccolo Original
Piccolo Books

Note to parents

The aim of these books is to encourage your child to do number work at home. Your attitude to the work is very important. If you are keen and enthusiastic about it, this will rub off on the child. Show an interest in what is produced and take time when you can to talk about an activity before the child starts. This will help to clear up misunderstandings and avoid mistakes. If a mistake is made, use it as a learning point rather than as a reason for criticism. If you are over-critical, you could put the child off altogether. Praise when you can but where there is an obvious lack of effort, say so.

The activities are designed to be interesting and enjoyable, since children learn best when they are interested and happy.

Concentration varies from child to child, but 10 to 20 minutes per session is a good guide. Watch out for signs of weariness and stop before the work becomes too boring.

The counting and writing activities here should come after the child has counted lots of real things in the real world. Whenever there are signs of confusion, go back to familiar objects (such as buttons, flowers, cups and so on) to clear up the problem.

Count the people in the queue.

How many?

Who is 2nd? ....

Who is 9th? ....

Who is 4th? ....

Ann is ....

Tom is ....

Jo is ....

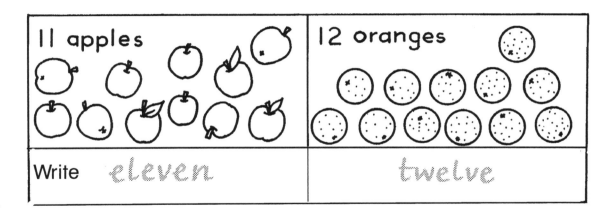

11 apples

12 oranges

Write *eleven*   *twelve*

3

Fill in the missing numbers.

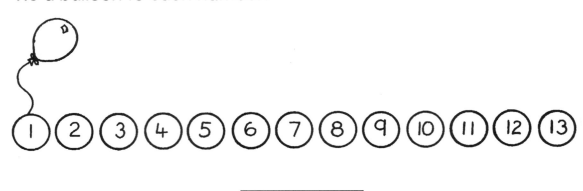

0   2   4   6   8   10   12   14   16

Tie a balloon to each number.

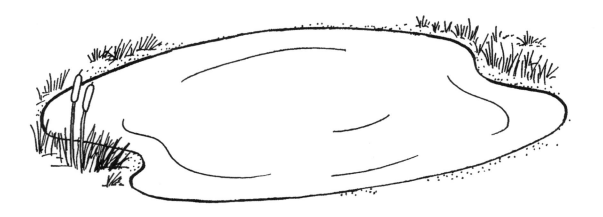

① ② ③ ④ ⑤ ⑥ ⑦ ⑧ ⑨ ⑩ ⑪ ⑫ ⑬

How many balloons? ◻

Draw thirteen tadpoles in this pond. Colour ten of them black and three of them brown.

Copy.

ten   and   three   makes   thirteen

Draw fourteen socks on this washing line.

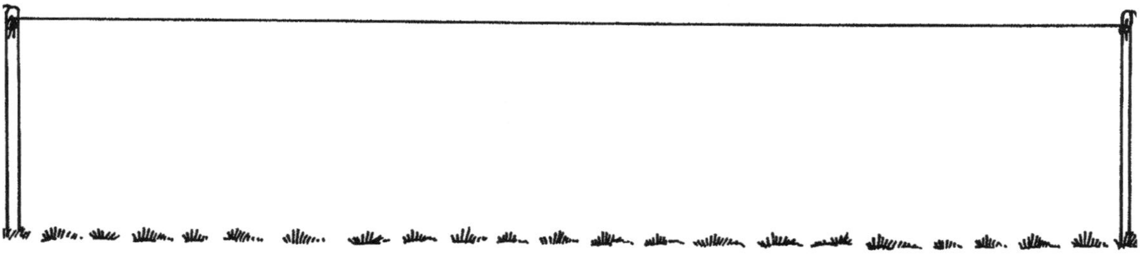

Write a number line to 15.

0

What is the number before 14?

What is the number after 14?

Count, colour then write.

14 balls 	15 straws 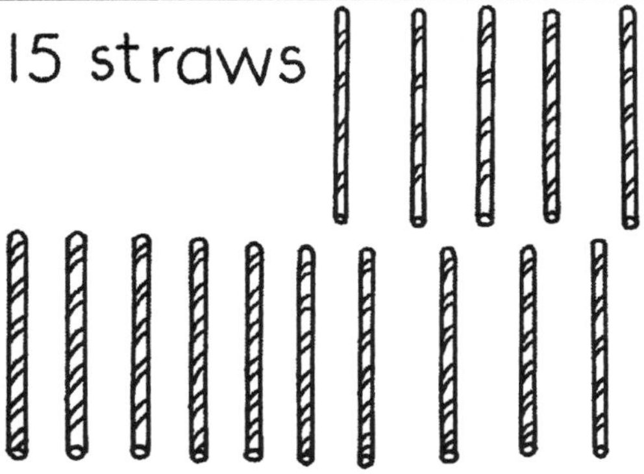
fourteen	fifteen

Copy. _____ _____

Complete the 'add one' arrows to 14 and fill in the missing numbers.

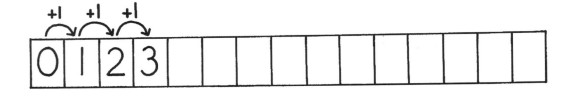

Can you do these sums?

4 add 1 ⟶ ☐   7 add 1 ⟶ ☐

3 add 1 ⟶ ☐   8 add 1 ⟶ ☐

6 add 1 ⟶ ☐   2 add 1 ⟶ ☐

5 add 1 ⟶ ☐   9 add 1 ⟶ ☐

Count the bricks and write the total in the top box. Now draw one more brick and write the new total in the bottom box.

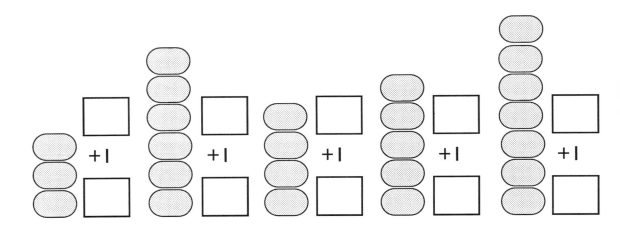

'Adding on one' is the same as saying <u>one more than</u>.
Put <u>one more</u> bead on each string. How many now?

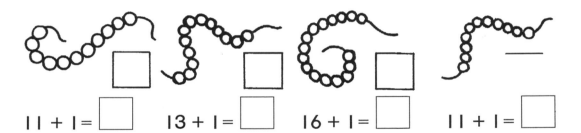

11 + 1 = ☐   13 + 1 = ☐   16 + 1 = ☐   11 + 1 = ☐

Complete the number line.

0   3 4   7   13   16   19 20

Use the number line to find out

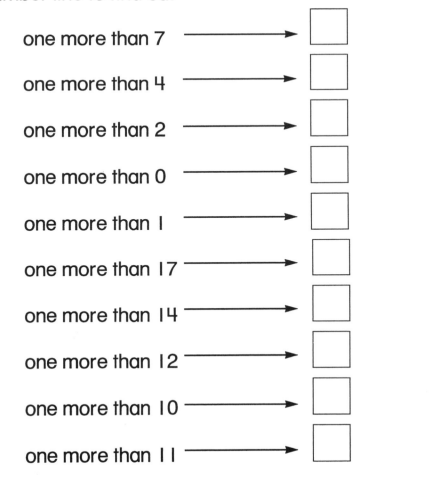

one more than 7 ⟶ ☐

one more than 4 ⟶ ☐

one more than 2 ⟶ ☐

one more than 0 ⟶ ☐

one more than 1 ⟶ ☐

one more than 17 ⟶ ☐

one more than 14 ⟶ ☐

one more than 12 ⟶ ☐

one more than 10 ⟶ ☐

one more than 11 ⟶ ☐

Complete the number line, then count aloud up and down.

←

15 16 17

●──●──●──●──●──●──●──●──●──●──●──●──●──●──●──●──●──●──→

What is the number before 16? ☐

Colour.

16

What is the number after 16? ☐

Start at the first box and tick sixteen boxes.

Start at the first box and tick seventeen boxes.

Count, colour, then write the number words.

16 flowers

17 flowers

sixteen

seventeen

Copy.

_____   _____

Add ten to all the numbers in the bottom line to complete the numbers to 20.

1	2	3	4	5	6	7	8	9	10
1	2	3	4	5	6	7	8	9	20

Colour ten balls. How many are left?

How many balls altogether?

Copy the sum.

10 + 4	⟶	14
4 + 10	⟶	

Do the sum.

Colour ten balloons. How many are left?

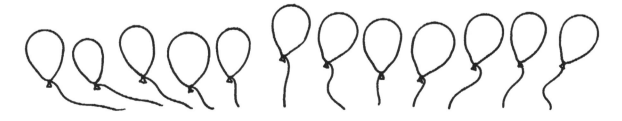

How many balloons altogether?

9

Colour ten lemons. How many are left?

How many lemons altogether?

Copy the sum.

10 + 5	⟶	15
	⟶	
5 + 10	⟶	

Do the sum.

Draw more flowers to make this into a bunch of thirteen flowers.

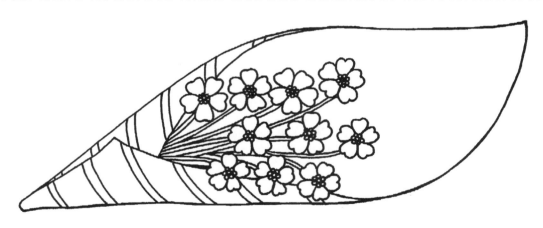

How many flowers did you draw?

Do the sums.

10 + 3	⟶	
3 + 10	⟶	

Start at 8 and fill in the missing numbers, then count all the numbers aloud.

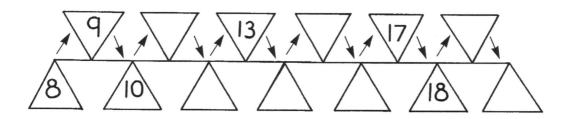

Write the number before 18.

Write the number after 18.

Colour

Start at the first box and draw a number line to 19.

Eighteen or nineteen? Use the number line to help you to answer the sums.

10 + 9 = ☐   19 + 0 = ☐

10 + 8 = ☐   18 + 0 = ☐

18 + 1 = ☐   11 + 8 = ☐

17 + 2 = ☐   11 + 7 = ☐

Complete the 'one less' arrows and fill in the missing numbers.

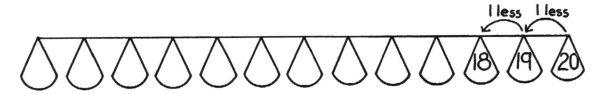

Can you do these sums?

one less than 13 ⟶ ☐   one less than 6 ⟶ ☐

one less than 12 ⟶ ☐   one less than 4 ⟶ ☐

one less than 10 ⟶ ☐   one less than 5 ⟶ ☐

one less than 9 ⟶ ☐   one less than 7 ⟶ ☐

Count the coins and write the total in the top box. Now cross one out. How many now? Write the total in the bottom box.

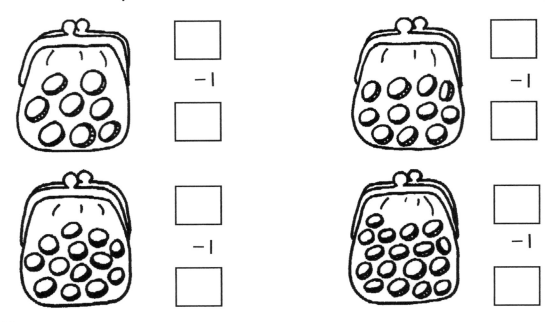

'One less than' is the same as saying <u>take one from</u>.
Cross out one apple from each bowl. How many now?

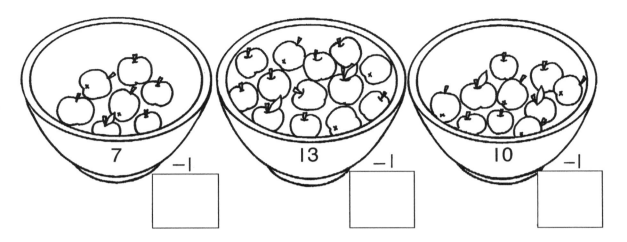

7   −1 ☐

13   −1 ☐

10   −1 ☐

Start from 16 and fill in the rest of the number line.

16

Take one from each number.

9 $\xrightarrow{-1}$ ☐   2 ⟶ ☐   12 ⟶ ☐

5 ⟶ ☐   19 ⟶ ☐   10 ⟶ ☐

4 ⟶ ☐   15 ⟶ ☐   17 ⟶ ☐

14 ⟶ ☐   12 ⟶ ☐   3 ⟶ ☐

Start at 20 and fill in the missing numbers.
The numbers in triangles are even. The others are odd.
Colour all the odd numbers green.

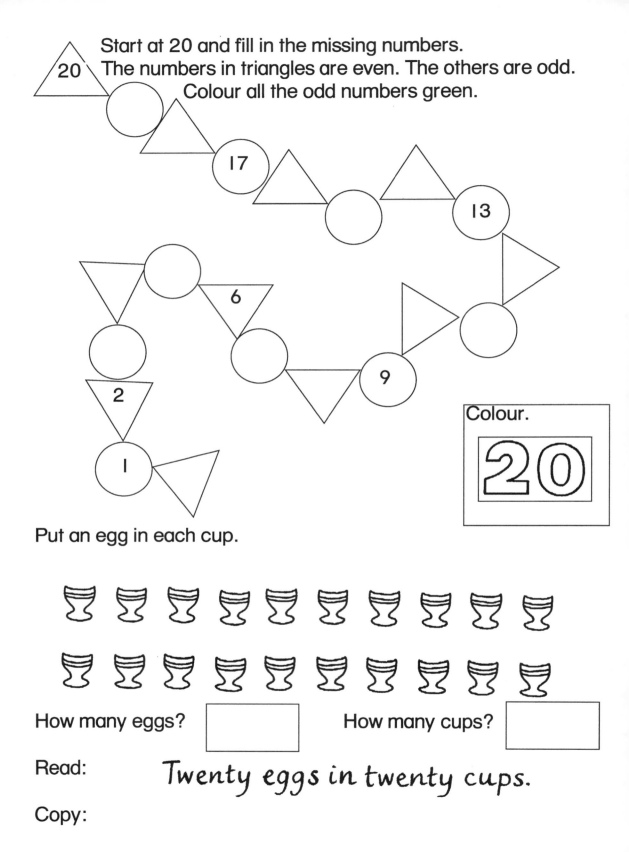

20

17

13

6

2

9

1

Colour.

20

Put an egg in each cup.

How many eggs? [ ]   How many cups? [ ]

Read: Twenty eggs in twenty cups.

Copy:

Count, colour, then write.

20 balloons

twenty balloons

Copy

10 balloons

ten balloons

Colour the number cards which come between 10 and 20.

11   3   6   20

9   14   1   18

7   10   12   8

What number comes <u>before</u>?

	18

	4

	7

	12

	10

	13

	20

	5

	6

Count the flowers. How many?

Colour the first flower red.
Colour the 4th flower blue.
Colour the 11th flower pink.
Colour the 8th flower yellow.
Colour the 6th flower green.

third

second

first

Copy.

Colour the second person.

Draw a number line to 16. Start at nought and circle every <u>second</u> number.

● ● ● ● ● ● ● ● ● ● ● ● ● ● ● ● ●
0 1 2

Put even numbers on the doors of these houses.

Put odd numbers on the doors of these houses.

Draw an even number of sweets in each bag.
Write the number of sweets you have drawn.

Colour all the circles. Count the circles then join them with a pencil line.

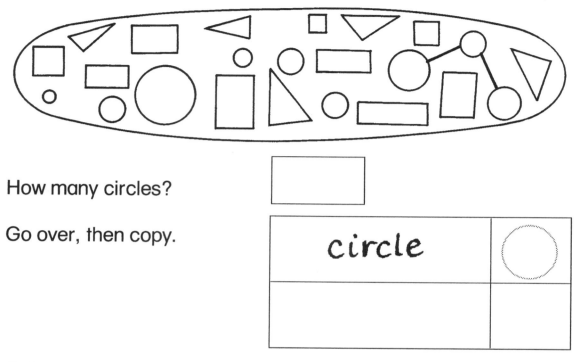

How many circles?

Go over, then copy.

circle

Colour all the squares. Count the squares then join them together with a pencil line.

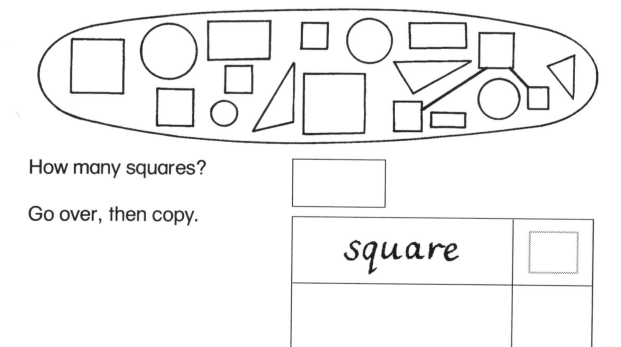

How many squares?

Go over, then copy.

square

Here is a set of twelve circles. Draw one more.

How many now?

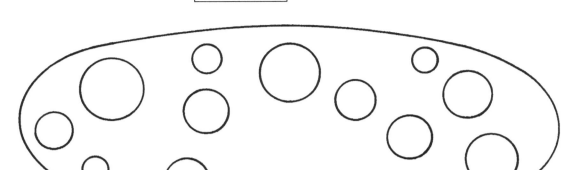

Copy the sum about this picture.

Here is one square. Draw twelve more. Count the squares.

How many now?

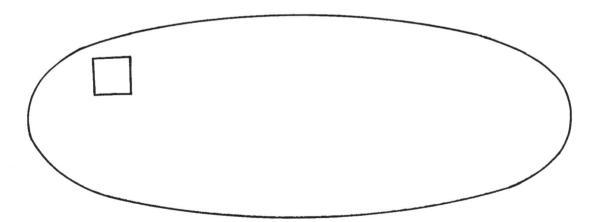

Copy the sum about this picture.

Colour all the triangles. Count the triangles then join them together with a pencil line.

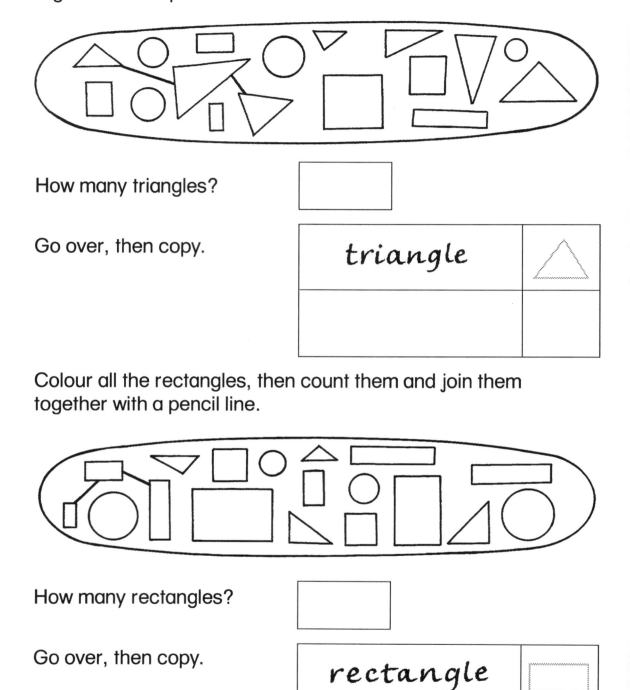

How many triangles?

Go over, then copy.

triangle	△

Colour all the rectangles, then count them and join them together with a pencil line.

How many rectangles?

Go over, then copy.

rectangle	▭

Here is a set of 13 triangles. Cross one out and colour the rest.

How many triangles did you colour?

Copy the sum about this picture.

13 − 1 ⟶ 12

Draw a set of 15 rectangles. Now cross one out and colour the rest.

How many rectangles did you colour?

Copy the sum about this picture.

15 − 1 ⟶ 14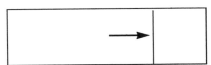

Put triangles round the odd numbers and circles round the even numbers. Count aloud the odd numbers, then the even numbers.

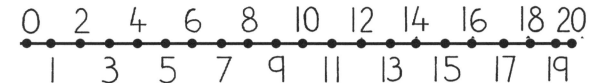

Fill each bag with an odd number of sweets. Write the numbers of sweets you have drawn.

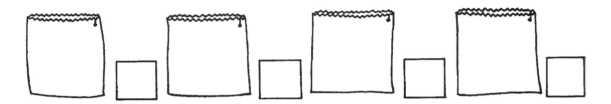

Draw $\overset{+2}{\frown}$ arrows to 12 and count aloud 'nothing add two is two', 'two add two is four'.

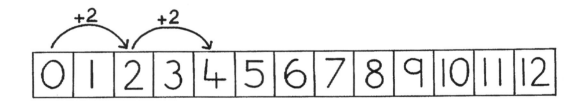

Write even or odd under these numbers.

Complete the number line.

Can you do these sums?

2 add 2	⟶	☐
4 add 2	⟶	☐
6 add 2	⟶	☐
8 add 2	⟶	☐
10 add 2	⟶	☐
12 add 2	⟶	☐

1 add 2	⟶	☐
3 add 2	⟶	☐
5 add 2	⟶	☐
7 add 2	⟶	☐
9 add 2	⟶	☐
11 add 2	⟶	☐

Colour the badges which have odd numbers.

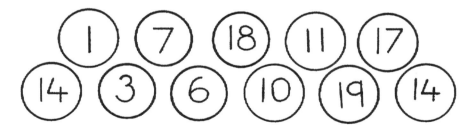

Fill in the missing links in the chain.

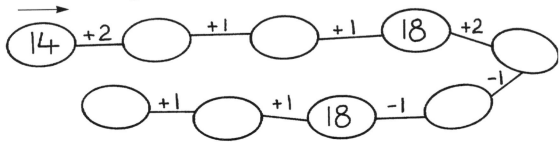

Draw −2 arrows and count down the number line.

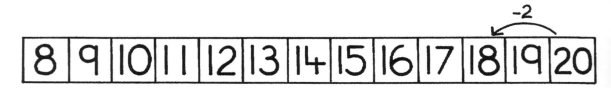

Take away two means the same as <u>less two</u>. Can you do these sums?

19 $\xrightarrow{\text{less 2}}$ ☐   12 $\xrightarrow{\text{less 2}}$ ☐

9 $\xrightarrow{\text{less 2}}$ ☐   2 $\xrightarrow{\text{less 2}}$ ☐

14 $\xrightarrow{\text{less 2}}$ ☐   16 $\xrightarrow{\text{less 2}}$ ☐

4 $\xrightarrow{\text{less 2}}$ ☐   6 $\xrightarrow{\text{less 2}}$ ☐

Count the buttons in each set then write the number in the top box. Cross out two buttons from each set. How many now? Write the new total in the bottom box.

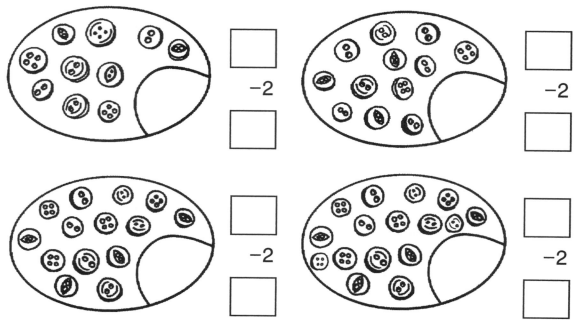

Finish the number chains.

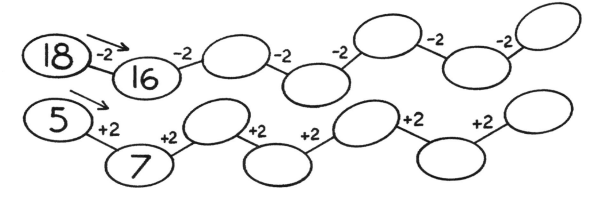

Colour half the shapes in each set red and the other half blue.

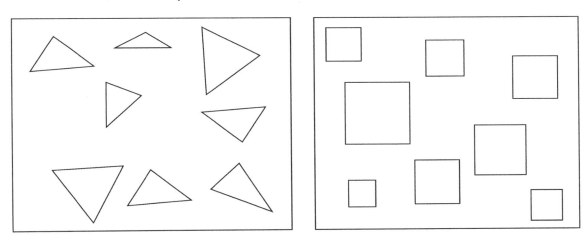

Colour the boxes which have even numbers.

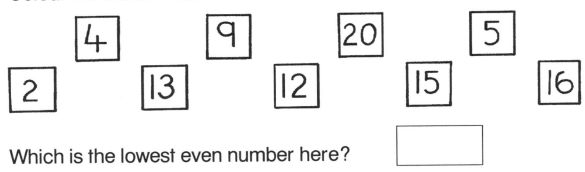

Which is the lowest even number here?

Which is the highest odd number here?

What number comes in the middle?

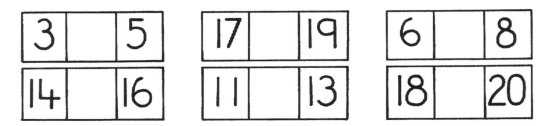

Write the number which is <u>one less</u> than

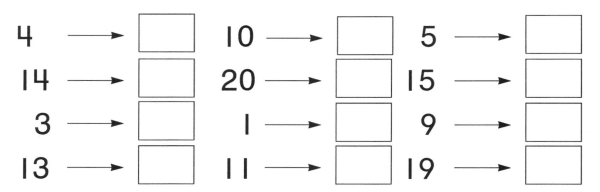

4 ⟶ ☐   10 ⟶ ☐   5 ⟶ ☐
14 ⟶ ☐   20 ⟶ ☐   15 ⟶ ☐
3 ⟶ ☐   1 ⟶ ☐   9 ⟶ ☐
13 ⟶ ☐   11 ⟶ ☐   19 ⟶ ☐

Complete the number chains.

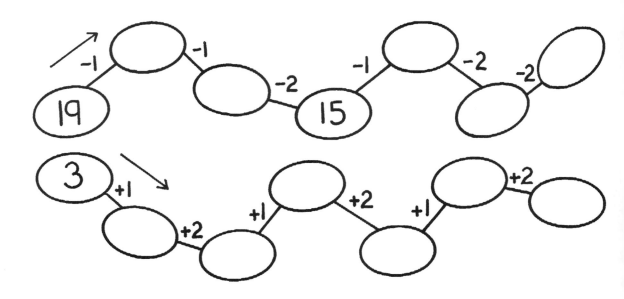

Go up the street and put <u>odd</u> numbers on the doors.

Come down the street and put <u>even</u> numbers on the doors.

What number comes <u>before</u>?

	17			13			20

	14			18			11

What number comes <u>after</u>?

7			3			10	

4			8			1	

Give each number a partner which is <u>one more</u>.

11			2			8	

19			16			7	

Complete these numbers to 20.

1	2	3	4	5	6	7	8	9	10
11				15					

Add the ten spots in the rectangle to the number of spots in each circle, then write the answer.

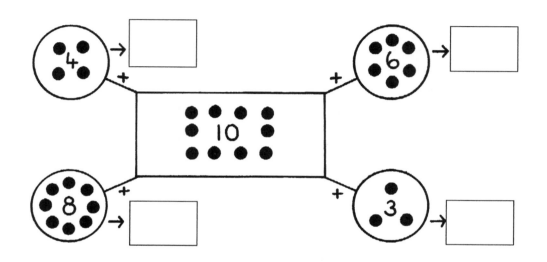

Can you do these sums?

10 + 5 ⟶ ☐   10 + 1 ⟶ ☐

10 + 2 ⟶ ☐   10 + 7 ⟶ ☐

10 + 3 ⟶ ☐   10 + 6 ⟶ ☐

10 + 9 ⟶ ☐   10 + 10 ⟶ ☐

Count the grapes in each bunch, then cross out 10.
How many now? Write the sum underneath. The first one
has been done for you.

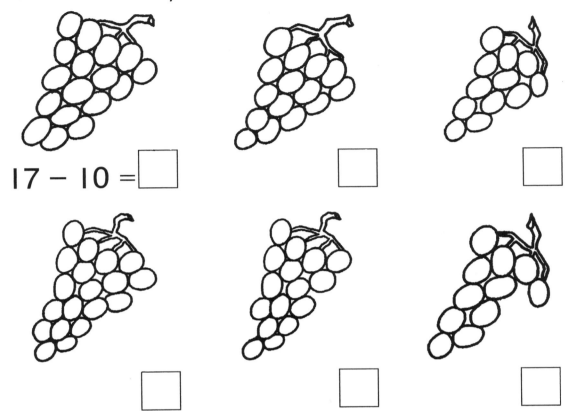

$17 - 10 =$ ▢

▢   ▢

▢   ▢   ▢

Fill in the missing numbers.

$10 + 5$ ⟶ ▭ $10 + 1$ ⟶ ▭

$10 + 2$ ⟶ ▭ $10 + 7$ ⟶ ▭

$10 + 3$ ⟶ ▭ $10 + 6$ ⟶ ▭

$10 + 9$ ⟶ ▭ $10 + 10$ ⟶ ▭

Read the top number chain aloud, then fill in the numbers in the bottom chain.

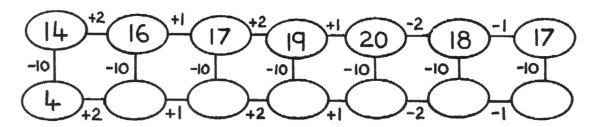

Fill in the number names to finish the sum.

Ten and _____ make eighteen.

Ten and four make _____

Fifteen take away ten is _____

Three and _____ make thirteen.

Ten and _____ make sixteen.

Ten and _____ make twelve.

_____ and ten make nineteen.

Read aloud the numbers on these vests. Now add ten to each number and read the new number aloud.
Colour the vests.

Write the numbers before and after.

Ten pigs are in this field. Can you draw more pigs to make twenty altogether?

Write. twenty pigs

What is?

2 less than 4 ⟶ ☐   2 less than 14 ⟶ ☐

1 more than 15 ⟶ ☐   1 more than 5 ⟶ ☐

2 less than 12 ⟶ ☐   2 less than 2 ⟶ ☐

2 more than 8 ⟶ ☐   2 more than 18 ⟶ ☐

1 less than 20 ⟶ ☐   1 less than 10 ⟶ ☐

Join the dot to dot to make the pictures.

Start at nought and go up in even numbers.

0

•12

4   14

6•

.2_____.10

•8

Start at twenty and count back in ones.

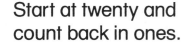

•1
•2
•3
20•   •4

19• ‗‗‗ •5

‗‗

18•   •6

17• 16 15 12 9 8 •7
    14 13 11 •10

Start at one and go up in odd numbers.

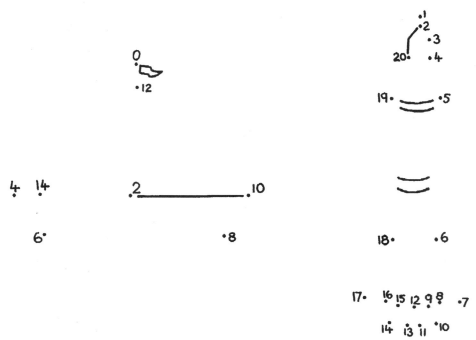

27   •25
      19•   •17
    •23 21•   •15

11• •9
13• •7 5

29•
1•
•3

Start at one and go up in ones.

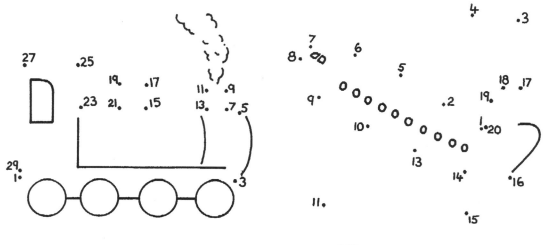

4
•3

7
8• ∞   6
      5
9• o o o   18 17
    o   o   •2 19•
10•   o o o   •20
      o o o
    13   14•   •16
11•
    •15
•12